AF255020

SELF CARE AT WORK

SELF CARE
AT WORK

How to Reduce Stress,
Boost Productivity, and
Do More of What Matters

Melissa Steginus

ISBN: 9781999265618 (paperback)

Learn about the author at:
www.melissasteginus.com

For the givers.

May your life and your work be blessed by
your self-care practice, and may you always
make time to give back to yourself.

CONTENTS

INTRODUCTION

Hi! I'm Melissa Steginus, mindfulness teacher and productivity coach. I'm also a counsellor, yoga instructor, entrepreneur, and writer. But I'm so much more than just job titles. And so are you.

This book is about us *as people*. Who are we outside of all of our roles, responsibilities, and to-do lists? Who are we *as ourselves?* And what do we do *for* ourselves?

Most people are familiar with the term "self-care." You have an idea of what it looks like (or could look like), and there's certainly no shortage of blog posts telling you what it *should* look like. But for most people (and this was certainly the case for me), that gap between knowledge and practice is wide. Huge, really. And maybe that's how it feels for you too.

I've structured this book to help you bridge that gap. If you want to start putting what you know about self-care, mindfulness, and healthy habits into practice (and seeing results!), this book is for you.

Knowledge may be power, but real change lies in action. In the *doing*. And in this book, you'll be doing a lot! You will:

- Identify your needs and goals

- Assess your current lifestyle (does it meet your needs and move you toward your goals?)

- Determine specific changes you want and maybe need to make

- Develop a plan to help you work more productively, fulfill your needs, and move toward goals that are meaningful to you

But that's only the beginning. The purpose of this book is to lay the foundation for a long-term self-care practice—something that is personal, purposeful, and practical.

That's why this book contains instructions for a personal project. In this project, you will:

- Create the foundation for your self-care action plan

- Develop ways to better manage stress and build healthy habits

- Determine the skills and tools you'll need for success (measured by consistency)

- Dive into your action plan to live out the changes that you want to see in your work, life, and self

The beauty of this book is that it's not over when it's over. Once you finish each chapter and have completed your project, you'll have a solid foundation for lasting change in your life.

Committing to your self-care is an investment in your well-being. Speaking from personal experience, this can directly benefit your productivity, the quality of your relationships, your ability to navigate and articulate thoughts and emotions, and so much more.

Whatever your role, schedule, or lifestyle, use this book to invest time and energy back into yourself, and transform the way you work and live.

It's time to start moving in the direction that's right for you.

CHAPTER ONE

BUILD YOUR PURPOSEFUL FRAMEWORK

Begin by asking yourself a few questions:

- What brought you to this book?

- What does productivity mean to you?

- Why is it important?

Of course, there are plenty of definitions out there, but as you will find in this book and with most things in life, creating your *own* definition keeps things purposeful and practical. This will make your progress much more meaningful in the long run because you'll (literally) be doing things on your terms.

Your personal definition becomes your framework. Your framework acts as the roots for your tree of growth, well-being, productivity, or whatever it is you want to invest in. Your roots are your purpose or your "why." Ask yourself *why* you want growth, well-being, productivity, etc. *Why* are you rooted in this?

It's your purpose that keeps you grounded and growing throughout your process. You can't grow a tree without roots!

You can't truly move forward if you don't know where you're going (or if you don't know why you're going in that direction). If that's the case, you're not really moving forward—you're just moving. It's like pushing papers or doing busy work; your hands are busy but you're not getting much accomplished.

But you're no paper-pusher, right? You're doing important work! You're aiming to get somewhere and nothing's going to stand in your way. Go, you! Just remember that if what you're doing lacks purpose or intention—if you don't know *why* you're working so hard to move in a certain direction—then all you're doing is losing energy.

We often set goals based on someone else's journey. We create ideals based on what we feel or are told we "should" do and where we "should" go. Then what happens? The goal becomes unattainable or we become apathetic because the roots are missing. That's because it was never *your* goal in the first place. It may have been practical for you, but it wasn't personal or purposeful so you kept pushing it to the bottom of the pile.

In order to see long-term success—and I define success in the context of self-care and personal growth as "consistent, intentional practice"— your framework will need three sides. Your definition of what you want to move toward must be personal, purposeful, and practical.

◆ ◆ ◆

**Success is consistent, intentional practice
leading to meaningful growth.**

Before we dive deeper...

Since this book is all about self-care for productivity and wellness at work, the examples I use will reflect a work context. But know that there is flexibility in what I teach—especially since you'll be customizing your framework and action plan to your lifestyle, needs, and goals.

If you're looking to explore productivity outside of a work context or you're substituting productivity with something else entirely, there will still be a *ton* of relevant information for you to take on and practice.

This is why creating your personal framework is so important. Take the reins! Grab this book by the horns! Make it work for you.

◆ ◆ ◆

Now let's shift back to those questions at the beginning of this chapter.

What brought you to this book?

It's pretty cool to think that any number of thoughts, feelings, and life events have led you to read these words in this moment. Of course, this path or series of paths differs greatly from person to person, and since I don't know you too well (yet), here's what I can piece together so far:

- You value productivity and want to increase yours

- You want to learn more about how your personal well-being impacts your work (and vice-versa)

- You want to create a plan that will benefit your well-being at work (and perhaps also in general)

- You're ready to take action to fulfill your needs and move toward meaningful goals

You make a great first impression! Let's keep getting to know each other, shall we?

What does productivity mean to you?

Whatever brought you to this book, consider how you define productivity. What does it look like to you?

Having worked with productivity experts and strategists and being trained in their coaching methods, I define it like this:

Productivity refers to both the action and the result of a process that centres on assessing one's priorities and then acting on them.

In this way, productivity applies to both how you do your work and how you measure it.

Consider how this definition encourages you to shift your perception of productivity from quantitative (how much or how many) to qualitative (how valuable). Rather than measuring your productivity by how much you're doing in a day or how many items you've checked off of your to-do list (quantitative), ask yourself, "What am I doing that *actually* matters to me?" (qualitative).

Why is productivity important?

Years ago, I was part of an event for Chris Guillebeau's *Born for This* book tour. In his talk about blending career and passion, Chris asked the audience a crucial question for assessing job fulfillment: "Did today matter?"

This question also holds weight when assessing your productivity. You may have checked 27 items off of your list for today, but did you get the *right* things done? What are you doing that matters to *you?*

To simplify our definition:

Productivity is purposeful doing.

It is paying *attention* to your *intention* to ensure that what you're doing is worth your time and energy. Will the outcome be worth your investment?

The "doing" will look different for each person depending on your job, lifestyle, routines, values, and so on. This is why it's up to you to define productivity for *your* goals and circumstances.

Remember

The root of productivity is in personal priorities. Know what matters to you and why. Put the purpose at the heart of your framework and you will be equipped and motivated to build meaningful, lasting habits.

Exercise

Take a minute to think about the three questions in this chapter before jumping to the next page. Jot down your answers to #2 and #3 on a sticky note, and keep this note in your planner, on your desk, or somewhere you will see it regularly.

CHAPTER TWO

REDEFINE SELF-CARE ON YOUR TERMS

So far, we've determined that productivity is a process (and outcome) of purposeful doing. This means investing in activities, roles, and practices that actually matter to *you*.

In the previous chapter, you defined productivity for yourself and assessed its importance in your life. Congratulations! You're more productive already. And we're only just getting started.

Now, you might be wondering what role does self-care play in all of this? Think of yourself as a vehicle, and your work (or life) is the road. Sometimes you're on the straight and narrow. Other times, your road twists, turns, or even circles back a time or two.

Self-care is your fuel through all of this. Whatever the road ahead or the path you've taken, self-care is what keeps your motor running and your wheels turning.

One of the main reasons I began writing about and teaching self-care is because it's a topic that's often brought up and brushed off as nothing more than a buzzword. As is true with most things, self-care isn't a universal "do this once and it'll change your life" deal. It's a self-care *practice*, after all.

I've found that self-care is often described as one of two extremes: survival or indulgence. It's presented as either drinking water and getting enough sleep or getting your nails done and going shopping. Of course you need water and sleep in order to keep your vehicle running (and, you know, stay alive). And sure, going shopping or getting your nails done might be a nice way to treat yourself now and then. But we need more than these two options on either end of the spectrum.

The good news is that self-care *is* the spectrum.

Self-care refers to a meaningful self-investment.

Like productivity, it is a practice of paying attention to your intention and doing things that matter to you.

◆ ◆ ◆

As we discussed in our last chapter, long-term success is defined by consistent and intentional practice. This requires that your self-care framework or action plan be personal, purposeful, and practical.

I reference these three pillars ("the three p's") frequently throughout the book, and we'll dive deeper into the specifics around each one in chapter five. For now, here's a quick introduction to each pillar so you have a better idea of what I'm referring to.

Personal

Self-care starts with self-awareness. Begin by learning how to tune into yourself, and then practice this regularly. How do you feel? What do you want or need?

Purposeful

Self-care strives for self-fulfillment. This is your "why" or the roots of your tree. How can you meet your needs and wants? How can you fuel or nourish yourself?

Practical

Activities that cultivate self-awareness (personal) and fulfillment (purposeful) will only continue to fuel you if you can continue to practice them. The key here is integration. What personal and purposeful activities can you integrate into your lifestyle? What can you do *regularly* to stay fuelled and fulfilled?

Exercise

Just as you did for productivity, spend a few minutes now creating your own definition for self-care. But before you dive in, let's zoom out to why you're here: for wellness at work.

Remember that work and life coexist. Wellness at work follows you home and vice-versa. The same goes for when you're *not* well, fuelled, or fulfilled. Work and life aren't opposing forces to balance; they go hand-in-hand and are intertwined as different elements of the same person: *you.*

So when creating your definition of self-care, consider your wellness both at work and outside of it. And know that the benefits of your self-care action plan will extend far beyond the walls of your workplace.

Going forward in this book and in life in general, you'll gain knowledge about self-care, productivity, and how these fit within your lifestyle. Your definition can (and likely will) change as your needs, wants, work, and life change. And that's okay, because you're going to create an action plan that will be simple and flexible enough to adapt to these changes.

Start with a definition that aligns with your current lifestyle. What does self-care look like for you now? What do you want it to look like? Why is it important?

Once you've jotted down your definition, flip to the next chapter, and let's explore the role of a self-care practice in making you more productive.

CHAPTER THREE

HOW SELF-CARE SHAPES PRODUCTIVITY

The idea of creating your own definition and framework actually takes into account the first step I teach when it comes to self-care: building awareness. In order for you to determine what matters to you and to work with purpose and productivity, you have to check in with yourself first. Ask questions to gain awareness of what's important to you. Then, assess how to implement and prioritize those values in your day and life.

This process of introspection for awareness is at the root of both self-care and productivity. And no, this isn't a coincidence—it's because the two are intertwined. Let's break this down a bit further.

We've determined that your purpose is at the root of your long-term success. So how do you determine your purpose? What is at the root of the "why"?

Think about how you make decisions. You're going about your day-to-day until you face something new. It could be a challenge, but let's call it an opportunity. You assess this new opportunity, considering how it might impact your current circumstances. If you're like most people, you weigh the short-term (maybe also long-term) pros and cons and make your decision accordingly.

The common factor in every step of that decision-making process is the person making the decision. And that's where self-care comes in. You now know that awareness is at the root of self-care (it's essentially the first half of the word —awareness of your *self)*. With self-awareness and connection, your decision-making process is straight-forward, rational, and rooted in self-trust.

Without a healthy relationship with yourself, however, your decision-making will be entirely external. What might that look like? When that new opportunity comes flying through your window, your thought process will look a lot different if you lack self-awareness. You might ask yourself, "How do I know if I should I do this?" "How might accepting this opportunity impact my partner or my boss?" Or maybe, "What would my friends think if I passed this up?"

Of course, we naturally consider others' perceptions when we wrestle with major life decisions. This is because we don't exist in a vacuum; we impact and are impacted by the people involved in our lives. That said, it's important to remember that the decisions you make are *your* decisions. And without checking in with yourself and what *you* want or need, you'll find that you start doing your work and living your life for everyone but yourself. That's not productive, it's not sustainable, and it's certainly not fulfilling.

Let's go back to the good old days when self-care was in the picture. With a greater awareness of your personal wants and needs, decision-making becomes a whole lot easier and more meaningful. It's much easier to trust yourself to make a major decision when you trust yourself in general.

◆ ◆ ◆

The role of self-care in a productive workday and lifestyle isn't just about decision-making. It expands into wellness in general.

Think back to our analogy of you as the vehicle and self-care as your fuel. It's what you need to keep you going. Without it, you're likely to hit the brakes or (hopefully not) spin out of control.

This my smooth segue into stress and burnout. (And I don't mean burnout in the sense of spinning your wheels doing donuts in the parking lot.) Let's take a look at what causes stress and burnout, how they differ, and how you can assess your fuel levels.

Consequences of neglect

Many of us have what I call the "superhero delusion." This is the idea that you can do it all, save the world, and still be home for dinner. I mean, that sounds great, right? What could be bad about that?

This mentality and lifestyle often lead to:

- Stress: bodily or mental tension caused by any physical, mental, or emotional factor (internal or external)

- Compassion fatigue: emotional and/or physical erosion that occurs from lack of or inability to refuel and regenerate

- Burnout: physical or mental collapse caused by overwork or stress (burnout is also defined as the reduction of fuel or substance to nothing through use or combustion)

Burnout is the result of too much energy output and not enough energy self-invested. In other words, it's burning too much fuel than you've put in your tank.

But how did this happen? What might have caused this? Let's look at some of the possibilities within the workplace.

Causes of stress and burnout

- High expectations (others' and your own)

- Inability to set boundaries

- Pushing yourself too hard: physical, mental, and/or emotional demands

- Heavy workloads and long hours

- Time pressures

- Limited resources

- Competing priorities

- Organizational pressures

There can be a wide range of contributing factors. You might also add relationship issues, financial concerns, toxic work environment, and any number of other stressors. Some days, you just blink and it feels like you've gone from full to empty!

It's important to note that there's a big difference between stress and burnout. We all experience stress in one way or another. Burnout, on the other hand, is the result of a long, heavy build up of stress that's been repressed or ignored. It's the collapse, the breaking point, the feeling of just throwing your arms up and saying, "I'm done."

Your self-care plan and practice will help you manage everyday stressors and prevent you from getting to that breaking point. It starts with knowing what to look for (i.e., your warning signs).

Signs you're low on fuel

- Physical: fatigue, difficulty falling asleep, restlessness, headaches, changes in sleeping or eating habits, changes in libido, increased blood pressure, increased susceptibility to illness

- Emotional: mood swings, irritability, isolation, changes in communication patterns and other relationship dynamics, withdrawal, feeling helpless, inadequate, unmotivated, overwhelmed, vulnerable, fragile, unable to cope

- Mental: confusion, difficulty making decisions or problem-solving, memory blanks, ambiguous feelings, difficulty concentrating or paying attention

Self-care is your tool to combat these things by dealing with what's at the root of them. Ideally, your self-care practice will be proactive in helping to prevent these signs (if not, it can still help you reduce their severity). Your practice is your way to cope with the stresses in and outside of the workplace so that you don't go home and develop a nasty habit that might harm you or someone else.

Keeping yourself well is also your best method for working productively. Think about what your workday looks like when you're not feeling your best. Your energy is low, your ability to focus is even lower, and the quality of your work suffers. This might mean you're easily distracted or directing a bit too much energy towards social media, email, or just plain old paper-pushing.

Unhealthy habits and lifestyles reduce your productivity, cost your business (which, if you're self-employed, is costing you), and create cyclical patterns of behavioural dysfunction and general dissatisfaction.

Case study

Let's use a real life example, Sarah. Here's a compacted look at her current circumstances:

- She works 9 to 5 in an extremely fast-paced work environment
- Her mother is unwell so Sarah visits and cares for her outside of work
- Sarah's husband struggles to keep up with the kids when she is away in the evenings
- Sarah constantly feels guilty, frustrated, and

completely exhausted

- She is emotionally overwhelmed and has trouble sleeping, which affects her ability to focus

- Then, Sarah's boss calls her into his office due to a minor administrative error

How do you think Sarah responded? Given your current circumstances, how would you have handled that situation?

I use this case study to challenge the myth that self-care is selfish. *Really?* Does Sarah's well-being only affect Sarah? Of course not! Her personal wellness affects her family, friends, boss, coworkers, clients, and even the clerk at the grocery store or the barista at the café where she gets her coffee.

Your personal wellness is not only about you.

And know that by making a positive self-investment, you also benefit those around you. Life can come in waves. Your well-being affects (and is affected by) those waves through small ripples of self-care and the decisions you make.

Remember

The key to both self-care and productivity is focusing on the ripples that you control: your behaviours and decisions. Productivity is all about time and energy optimization, right? Paying attention to your intention. And self-care is exactly that, just in a bit of a different context. It's all about reinvesting energy into yourself so that you have energy to expend (to send outward in productive ripples and waves).

Building healthy habits at work and otherwise starts with awareness.

Know what *you* want, where *you* want to invest your energy, and *why*. The "why" determines the "how."

In the next chapter, we'll shift into the "how." You'll determine your starting point and assess various elements of your life and self.

Exercise

Before you dive into the next stage of this book, take a minute to reflect on your definitions of productivity and self-care. How will self-care help you manage those day-to-day stresses to prevent compassion fatigue and burnout? Who else is affected by your wellness?

Make any adjustments you feel are necessary to your framework before moving forward. Then, let's begin!

CHAPTER FOUR

IDENTIFY YOUR STARTING POINT

By this point, you've explored your definitions and needs surrounding productivity and self-care. You've also begun strengthening and deepening your personal awareness to lay the foundation for meaningful action. Essentially, you've begun sketching out a roadmap for yourself. You've thought about what kind of fuel your vehicle needs and what might provide you with that fuel.

Now it's time for the wheels to start turning—time to gain momentum and cover some ground. The pace might be slow at first, and that's fine. The key is to start from where you are and take one step at a time.

I stated in the introduction that this book is about us as people—you as a *person*. Who are you outside of your roles, responsibilities, and to-do lists? Who are you as yourself, and what do you do for yourself?

This is your time to begin to really think about these questions. Maybe you won't find the answers just yet, and that's okay! It's all part of the process. The point is to become more comfortable with introspection, especially when it comes to deep questions around who you are and what you want.

Think this is pretty deep for productivity? Well, yes and no. Learning how to be aware of and connected to yourself helps you identify and move toward your ideals in both work and life. This makes you a healthier individual and aligns you with your purpose—however you've defined that for yourself.

We've talked about the consequences of a lifestyle that lacks self-care—one overcome by stress, fatigue and eventually burnout. We've discussed the role of self-care in combating these things and also in making you more productive in work and in general. As we move forward, you'll begin to apply this information to you: your work, priorities, and lifestyle.

Identifying your starting point in this process begins with getting to know yourself as a person. It's a strange concept, getting to know yourself, but our relationships with ourselves are often clouded by what we do with and for others.

Think about how you introduce yourself or answer the question, "What do you do?" What's the first thing you respond with? Job titles. Family roles. Imagine how weird it would be if you asked someone what they did and they responded with, "I'm passionate about painting" or "I feel happiest when I'm building birdhouses." It would probably throw you off a bit.

We rarely share personal information with people right off the bat. It's much more professional and socially acceptable to start with a job title. And that's not necessarily an issue, but my point is that this practice of defining ourselves to others by what we do for *work* can make it increasingly harder to define ourselves outside of that box.

You and I both know that we as *people* are much more than what we do for work. So now it's time to practice thinking about yourself as a *person*. That's how you'll determine what matters to you, which determines your self-care practice, which then determines how you can be most productive.

How to check in with yourself

There are many areas of your life and yourself that make you who you are. Becoming familiar with your many facets will help you do self assessments or check-ins. This practice will help you identify your starting point (your lifestyle and current circumstances) and determine the areas that could use a little extra investment.

Use the following questions to try out a quick self-check-in. (Looking at each facet and its related questions, it might feel overwhelming to explore these ideas all in your head. Having a way to record your answers, like a notepad or journal, can be extremely helpful.)

- **P**hysical: what is your body telling you? If you're constantly tired or tense, is your body holding onto stress that you're not dealing with?

- **E**motional: how do you feel? Notice how you react to certain people or situations. (Think back to the example of Sarah who was exhausted and overwhelmed. How might that impact how she responded to criticism or confrontation?)

- **R**ational: what's your mentality? Are your thought patterns clear or clouded by worry, doubt, or negativity?

- **S**piritual: this might be rooted in beliefs, personal values, or self-connection. Do you feel connected to your purpose or a higher power? Are you living in accordance with your values?

- **O**ccupation: how are you performing at work? How is your job treating or serving you? And do your outcomes match the energy you put in?

- **N**etwork: what is the quality of your relationships? Are they mutual or one-sided? Who do you rely on for support?

These six areas (physical, emotional, rational, spiritual, occupation, and network) represent you as a PERSON. Give or take a few interpretations, they are the facets that make you *you*. Remember that you can adjust the name of each area as well as its questions so that your check-in is personal to you.

Another way to ask and explore these questions is with a wellness wheel. This exercise creates a visual representation of the areas of your life that you feel could use some extra attention. Over the next few pages, I'll show you a breakdown of what that exercise might look like.

Wellness Wheel Exercise

Step 1: Mark a point in the centre of your page and draw five concentric circles around it. Either around the circle or as a list underneath, write the six facets of your person: physical, emotional, rational, spiritual, occupation, and network. Your wheel will look something like the one below (numbers are optional).

Image 1:

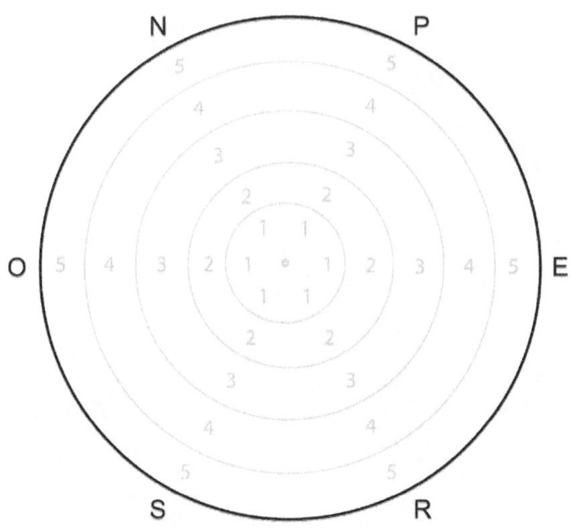

Step 2: Once you've drawn your circles, divide your wheel into six parts, and adjust the size of each "slice of the pie" according to the value you assign to each facet. Note that the wheel below is divided into six equal parts for reference—one for each element or facet. Nice and tidy, all equal sizes. You'll adjust the size of each section depending on its level of importance to *you* (see Image 3).

Image 2:

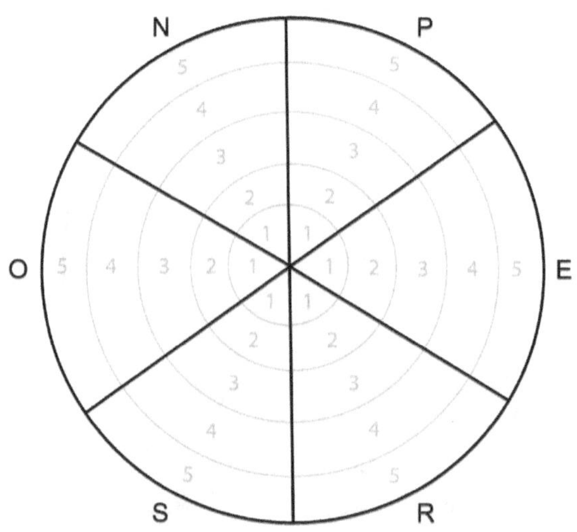

Most wheels will resemble the one below in the sense that not every area is equal in size. In this wheel, we see that physical and rational health as well as occupation are the main priorities as these sections are the largest.

Your values and interests will determine the level of importance (i.e., size) you assign each facet. Divide the sections of your wheel to make it relevant to you.

Image 3:

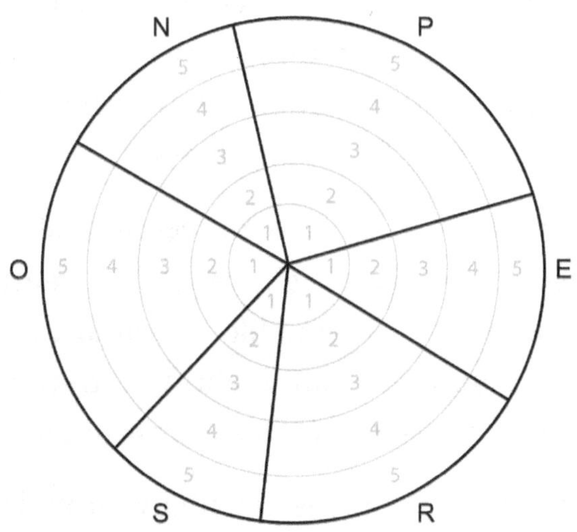

Step 3: Next, shade in each section according to your current level of satisfaction. Five means you're very satisfied, three is somewhat satisfied, and one indicates little to no satisfaction. If you feel physically healthy, for example, you might rate your satisfaction a four or five, and that section would be almost fully shaded. Do this for each section of your wheel.

If you're not sure how to measure your satisfaction with each section, you can assess these statements:

- Physical: I eat a balanced nutritional diet, I exercise at least three times per week, I have a healthy relationship with my body, I am generally free from illness

- Emotional: I am able to feel and label my feelings, I can express my feelings appropriately, I am able to comfort myself when upset, I can identify and practice healthy ways to cope with stress or anger

- Rational: I pursue mentally stimulating interests or hobbies, I have positive thoughts and self-talk, I commit time and energy to learning and self-development

- Spiritual: I have a general sense of serenity or self-connection, I have faith in a higher power or deeper consciousness, I have a sense of meaning and purpose in my life, I respect life's mysteries and can be present in certain moments

- Occupation: I find meaning or satisfaction in what I do at work, my work allows me to gain important skills or do things that matter to me, I have a solid work-life harmony, I feel valued and respected at work, I perform well at work and give my best effort to what I do or make

- Network: I am aware of others' feelings and respond appropriately, I resolve conflicts with others calmly and empathetically, I have close trusting relationships, I am able to set and respect my own and others' boundaries

Once you've shaded each section based on your level of satisfaction, your wheel might look something like the one below. In this example, you can see that the areas of greatest importance also show the levels of highest satisfaction (a good sign but certainly not always the case).

Note: be honest and gentle with yourself in these two final steps. The goal for right now is simply to identify your starting point.

Image 4:

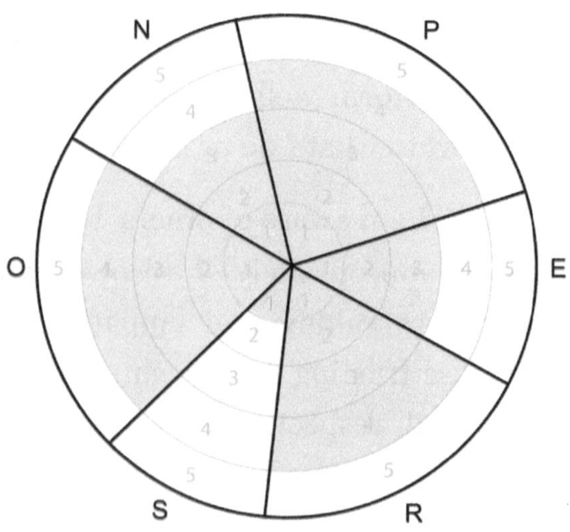

Step 4: Finally, write your current level of investment on the parameter of each section. Choose a number from one to five that you feel reflects the amount of time, energy, and attention you *currently* invest into that area of your life. Again, the higher the number, the greater your current level of investment.

Once complete, you'll have your wellness wheel and your starting point for your action plan.

Image 5:

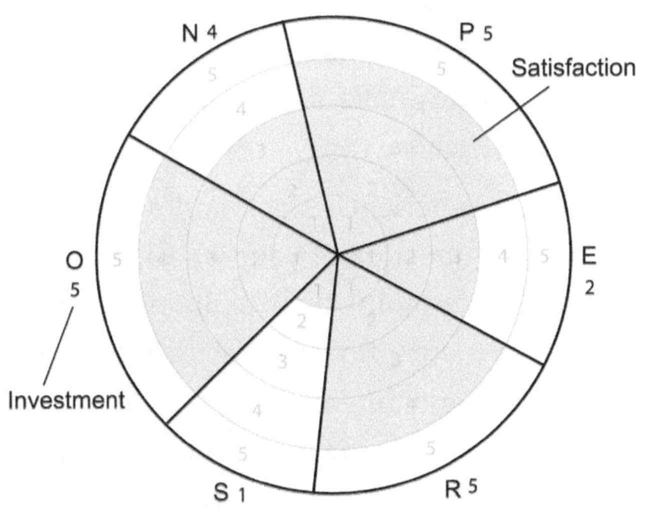

Remember

Keep in mind that this exercise isn't intended to be a blow to your ego. The purpose here is to note and visually *see* where you send your energy and which areas are lacking.

When energy lacks in an area you deem important (the larger sections of your wheel), you experience imbalance, dissatisfaction, and decreased productivity. It's like when you get sick and your body feels like it's forcing you back to bed so you can rest. Your body is trying to get back into balance. Or think about driving with a flat tire. Your vehicle knows something's up, and it's not going to make it very far until you pay attention to what's wrong.

When you experience signs and symptoms of imbalance in one area of your wheel, you can be sure those symptoms will spill over into the others (hence our previous discussion on work-life harmony and interconnection). When your wellness wheel is in balance, your vehicle runs much more smoothly. *You* run much more smoothly. And that, my friend, is what productivity is all about.

Exercise

Consider what you've learned from your wellness wheel. How has this practice shed light on your current lifestyle? What do you want your wheel to look like? Before moving forward, take a few minutes to highlight the area(s) you'd like to invest more energy into, and jot down what that might look like.

CHAPTER FIVE

THREE PILLARS OF A PRODUCTIVE PLAN

We've established your starting point through self-assessment and the wellness wheel exercise. You've pinpointed where you are on your roadmap, and now it's time to actually map out your route with an action plan.

As I've stated before, a successful plan or framework is one measured by consistent, intentional practice. And in order to create a lasting action plan, you'll need to make yours purposeful, personal, and practical.

Let's walk through this process and what each of these specific pillars might look like in practice.

Purposeful

A purposeful action plan answers the "why." Your purpose is your first question and your ultimate goal. It's what your plan is rooted in, and it's your marker to measure whether or not something is working.

In this book, you started with "why." Why do you want to be more productive? And you now have a personal definition of productivity and its purpose for you. Let's say your definition is to streamline your work processes to cut down on time spent in the office unnecessarily. The streamlining process is half the battle; the other half (the long term make-or-break) lies in what you do with the extra time you now have. If you save yourself an extra hour of work each day only to slump on your couch and watch an extra hour of TV, is there really a long term benefit? Or will you eventually tire of the extra time on the couch and default back to longer workdays?

On the other hand, let's say your definition of productivity is to streamline your processes to spend less wasted time in the office so that you can sit down and eat dinner with your family each night. Or maybe it's so you have the time and energy after work to further a personal project in the evenings. By clarifying your purpose or motivation and including it in your definition, you're more likely to build productive habits—and stick to them.

What you make time for—the activities, projects, and people you value—play an essential role in your well-being. Being more productive at work so you have more energy (or fuel) to invest outside of work becomes a cycle that fuels you. One might even dare to say it's a cycle of *productive self-care*. Whoa.

Now, let's take a step further to look at the activities and investments that fuel you. You're using that extra hour after work to eat with your family because, sure, you love your partner and your kids. But dig a little deeper. You spend that hour hearing about everyone's day, and you feel a deep sense of connection. You feel part of this interwoven network of human beings living both individually and interdependently. And that's pretty special! Maybe that's where your purpose lies.

Or let's say you use that extra hour each evening to further a personal project. Maybe you're writing a book, starting a business, or building birdhouses in your garage for no other reason than because it brings you joy. You're a passionate creator, and making something truly your own gives you purpose.

Whatever the activity (so long as it's healthy and it fuels you), it's an act of self-care. It's worth making time for. And (bonus!) it's making you more productive at work.

Personal

The second pillar of your lasting action plan is that it's personal. It's made by you and for you, which is why you've already spent time creating your framework—so that your action plan is tailored for your situation, your needs, and your ideals.

This book is all about moving and growing in *your* right direction. That's why there is no "should" here. You'll notice I don't tell you that you "should" do this, try that, follow this path. How can I tell you what you should do when I'm coming from a totally different place and potentially looking to move forward in a completely different direction?

We all have different starting points, directions, and modes of transportation. If you're looking to hike up a mountain, for instance, you aren't interested in what car you "should" buy to get you up that mountain because you want to hike. And if you're taking the scenic route by car, you aren't concerned with hiking gear because it doesn't pertain to your needs and desires. No one is universally right because there is more than one way up a mountain. And there is certainly more than one mountain.

Just focus on *your* mountain and *your* path— don't worry too much about what someone else says you "should" do. Know what you want to do and why it's important to you. Why is it important *to you* to be productive? Why is it important *to you* to practice self-care? How will you use these practices to help you get up *your* mountain?

Earlier in this book, we talked about how self-care impacts your decision-making process. We went through the downfalls of making decisions externally—that is, based on everything and everyone else. Think about this as if you're heading up a windy mountain without a map of your route. No markers, no path, just you. You might consider taking a moment to gather your bearings, identify where you are, and create a route for yourself. But instead, you hear a voice in the distance telling you where you should go, what steps you should take, and what your journey should look like. What do you do? Who do you listen to? Do you create a path based on where you know you are or do you listen to someone on a different route—possibly on a different mountain entirely?

When you paint the picture like that, the answer seems pretty simple, doesn't it? An action plan that's personal to you—your starting point, needs, desires, and so on—will keep you going much longer. And, more importantly, it will keep you going in the right direction because it's the direction that you've chosen for yourself.

Practical

The third and final pillar of your action plan lies in its practicality. Are you creating realistic goals and ideals? Do you have the tools and supports you need to move in a certain direction? If not, can you gather them? No? Then what other options do you have?

This branches off of our previous pillar: making your plan personal. If the self-care activities you want to practice aren't practical, then how can your plan be tailored to you? If your definition of productivity is rooted in office life and suddenly you're at home raising twins, your definition and approach will need to change to reflect your new needs and lifestyle.

When thinking of self-care ideas and activities,

ask yourself: is this an activity I can maintain? When I'm stressed or frustrated at work, can I do this activity? When I'm starting my morning or winding down in the evening, can I do this activity?

Remember, these activities don't have to be revolutionary. Self-care can be closing your eyes and taking a few deep breaths to dispel frustration. Maybe you keep a notebook by your desk and write down one sentence of gratitude each day. It could also look like a consistent exercise routine, a regular phone call with a friend, or a technology-free meal with your family (or yourself).

Keep things simple and practical so that an activity that fuels you doesn't become this massive, daunting obligation. Your self-care activity doesn't need to be yet another thing that lingers on your to-do list.

◆ ◆ ◆

So there you go. You now have three pillars for an effective, long-lasting action plan that's purposeful, personal, and practical. If you ever get lost in a whirlwind of thought, come back to your three pillars:

- Does this deepen your self-awareness? (Purposeful)

- Does this nourish and/or fulfill you? (Personal)

- Can you do this consistently? (Practical)

Your action plan is your roadmap. It helps you get the wheels in motion, and it steers you toward long-term success: consistent, intentional practice. This is your path to creating and sustaining healthy habits that fuel you to keep going.

Exercise

Before moving on to the next chapter, take another look at your wellness wheel. Based on your levels of satisfaction and investment, ask yourself a few questions:

- Where would you like to focus a little extra energy?

- What do you want (or need) from your self-care practice?

- Based on your pillars, what can you do to start practicing self-care today? How can you start fuelling yourself now and move in the direction that's right for you?

We've covered a lot of big picture stuff up until this point. In the next chapter, we'll funnel all of these concepts into immediate and specific action so you can start to see what this process looks like in practice. Gear up (or should I say gear down), because the next chapter is a lot of work as the uphill climb begins.

Let's move forward together to put your plan into action.

CHAPTER SIX

THE PROCESS: FROM PLAN TO PRACTICE

Welcome to the action chapter of this book! By this point, you've already taken a number of steps toward a more intentional and productive lifestyle. Let's review:

- You redefined productivity and self-care in ways that are purposeful, personal, and practical

- You outlined your framework—in terms of both work and lifestyle

- You checked in with yourself using the PERSON acronym to identify your needs, wants, and ideals

- You determined the changes you want to

- make and where you want to invest more energy

- You explored the role self-care can (and will) play in your productivity, and you outlined a few specific activities you can start practicing right away

In this chapter, you'll take these pieces and put together your puzzle. It's time to start integrating your action plan into your day-to-day life—both in the office and outside of it. As you move forward, remember that the progress is in the process. You are creating a system for yourself, an ongoing practice to keep you fuelled and performing well. This isn't about achieving a certain goal though goal-setting can certainly be used within your system. The only goal is to build a structure for your self-care practice so you can develop and lean on healthy, productive habits. And that is certainly a process.

Before you begin, lay everything out on the table in front of you. I mean literally, everything we've discussed this far: your definitions and framework, your wellness wheel, the self-care activities you've outlined, and any notes you've taken on what's stood out for you. Keep all of that within an arm's reach.

Second, let's dive in. You used the wellness wheel to get an idea of your big picture needs, wants, and ideals. Now, let's move into a different kind of assessment: your day-to-day schedule. Needless to say, your process will look different than mine, but I want to walk you through what I've done for myself to create a purposeful, personal, and practical self-care practice that makes me *infinitely* more productive. Of course, feel free to take on or adapt my process if/where it fits with your path.

◆ ◆ ◆

Back in 2012, I did the wellness wheel exercise for the first time. My wheel was off-balance to say the least with about 50% of my time and energy dedicated to education and 50% to my occupation. You can imagine what my lifestyle looked like: overworked, highly stressed, frequently sick, and spending very little time with friends and family.

Once I completed my university degree, I faced a lot of anxiety because a big chunk of my wheel was now missing. And I knew I didn't want to fill it with more work. I wanted to pump some air into the other areas (my flat tires) so that I could create more balance for myself.

For those who struggled with the wellness wheel exercise, I'm well aware that it can feel sad and frustrating. I've been there. But after looking at my wheel, I knew I had to change something. Well, a lot of things... but one thing at a time.

I took the steps you've already taken throughout this book: I redefined self-care and productivity, asked myself a series of tough questions, built my framework, and gained a deeper understanding of what I actually wanted things to look like and why.

Then I put what I learned into action. Here's what I did (and where you'll jump back in).

Schedule yourself into your day

Set a meeting with yourself and *keep* it. Make it a priority. Treat that meeting like you would any other. It doesn't have to be one or two hours either. Start with 15 minutes in the morning or on your lunch break. Use that time to practice one activity you set in your action plan: a walk, a phone call with a friend, a journal entry, or a quick yoga practice or series of stretches.

Set a consistent time each day for your meeting, and put it in your calendar. Whether you use a paper or digital calendar, block off your 15 minutes, close your door, mark yourself busy —do whatever you have to do to spend that time by yourself, for yourself.

When finding a consistent space for your self-care practice, start with what you know. This method works whether you're set in a 9 to 5 schedule, navigating through shift work, or creating your own schedule as a freelancer. I've done it with each of these schedules. Some are easier than others, of course, but it's definitely doable within each one.

Let's break down what this might look like within the context of a "traditional" 9 to 5 office job. Meeting with colleagues, managers, and clients constitutes your fixed time—that which is set each week (and may be set for you). That time is blocked off and won't be going anywhere. You could consider blocking off a 30- or 60-minute lunch break as well to ensure that you're not tempted to work through it. (In previous jobs where I had flexible breaks, I kept my lunch hour fixed and consistent for myself and to set clear boundaries with both clients and coworkers.)

Your fixed time can also include events, appointments, and commitments you have outside of work. Do you regularly attend an exercise class in the evenings or early mornings? My calendar, for example, includes a health and self-care label for exercise classes, mindful morning routines, community events, and weekly phone calls with friends and family. By scheduling your self-care, you build the habit of setting aside time for yourself and your community. That way, you're both available for and actively seeking out these opportunities.

Map out any regular commitments that have that fixed time block. Whether it's set in stone or not, putting it in your schedule sets an expectation that you are committed to something (or someone) and will set that time aside.

That leaves flexible and free time. Flexible time is for important commitments that aren't time-specific. This might include exercise, household chores, walking the dog, grocery shopping, meal planning, etc. These are things you want and need to do but not necessarily at 4:15pm on a Tuesday.

What's left is your free time. Even with a seemingly full schedule, you can (and hopefully do) still have a bit of wiggle room. Avoid hyper-scheduling yourself so you have free time to do something creative or perhaps to do nothing at all. And remember to use at least one free 15-minute increment in your day to practice and expand your self-care activities.

As you go about revamping your scheduling,

treat it as an experiment, knowing that it's a starting point, and your calendar will grow and change as you do.

Stack your habits

Habit stacking is a popular topic in the productivity realm. And it's important because it focuses on the big picture: the system or overarching process. The goal is not necessarily to hit a certain target like being able to practice five self-care activities in your 15 minutes. Like productivity, self-care is *qualitative*, not quantitative. Focus on the meaning and intention behind your activity. The purpose behind the practice.

Contrary to popular belief, productivity isn't about how much you can do. It's about whether or not you're doing the *right* things—the things that matter to your work and to *you*. And that means starting small with what you know matters to you.

If you work a high-stress job, you may want to

start with something that will help you reduce stress so you can maintain balance and prevent fatigue. For me, that's meant keeping a one-sentence gratitude journal that I write in at the beginning of each day. You might also consider using a planner or calendar to keep track of meetings and tasks. This helps you set and stick to boundaries so you don't double-book or hyper-schedule yourself. Maybe you have a 30- or 60-minute "closed door" policy for you to minimize distractions and get your work done instead of taking it home with you. Or maybe this looks like waking up 20 to 30 minutes earlier each workday to spend time meditating, reading, drawing, or learning about something outside of work.

Whatever the activity you choose, choose *one*. Practice it regularly—every day for one week, then two weeks, then a month. Once it becomes a habit and your routine feels weird without it, then (and only then!) consider how you can expand it. This is when you might start to explore other activities to add to that morning routine or to another part of your day. The process of habit stacking can be slow-going, but the key is to lay your foundation and ensure it's solid before building on it.

Track your process (to see your progress)

Finally, I want to touch on the importance of tracking and reviewing your process. Already, you may have noticed the value of reflection as you've practiced it throughout this book. Reflection goes hand-in-hand with assessment and leads to long-lasting growth and change (in combination with action, of course).

So what might this reflection look like? I don't know if you've ever been one for journalling, but that's one tool or method we'll explore in this book. Now, don't let the term "journalling" throw you off; there are many different ways to track and review what you're doing for self-care and how (or whether) it's benefiting you. Simply think of journalling as the process of documentation and review.

Review is essential to evaluation, which is essential to progress. Journalling is a great way to pay attention to "how it all came to be." In looking back, you gain insight into (and appreciation for) your challenges, lessons, and perseverance.

Journalling also helps you gain clarity on your current situation. How many times have you looked at your circumstances and wondered, "How did I get here?" or "What would things look like if I had done A instead of B?" Sometimes the answer is clear. Other times, not so much. By journalling, the odds are good that you could flip through the pages, add up a few events or decisions, and find the answer.

For example, you ask yourself, "How did I get here?" and you wonder about it. So you flip through the pages or scroll if you're into digital journalling. Then you see, "Well B led to C, and then D happened, which prevented me from doing A." And you might think to yourself, "Wow, I really miss doing A. I'm going to do some of that today."

You review the past to assess the present and then determine what actions are necessary to change your future. You take what you know and apply it to how you want to grow. Thus, the power of journalling.

Give it a try. Start by deciding your medium: digital or paper. Make this decision right off the bat and stick with it. Journalling is a practice of organizing jumbled thoughts, feelings, etc., and jumping back and forth between mediums is totally counterproductive.

Whether using a digital document, online app, or good old fashioned notebook, the key to journalling is to make it a habit—even if for a few minutes each day (and preferably at a similar time). I personally like journalling before I go to bed. This way, it's not just at the end of the workday but at the end of my entire day. There's so much to reflect on in life (outside of your workday) that affects and is affected by work.

If you had a great day, take a few minutes to celebrate that. If your day felt like an endless struggle and you're just waiting for it to be over, reflect on what made it challenging. Being specific puts things in perspective, transforms thoughts and feelings into practical actions, and can shed light on the problem should it arise again in the future.

Journalling can be a great way to track your self-care practice and how it impacts your productivity. Maybe you want to write about what you did during the 15 minutes you scheduled with yourself that day. What activity did you practice, how did it benefit you, and how can you continue to shape it into a habit? Or ask yourself, "How was my day today?" or "Did today matter to me?" Choose up to three questions that matter to you. Again, keep things personal, purposeful, and practical.

Remember

Meaningful, long-lasting change doesn't happen overnight. Be patient with yourself, and know that the progress is in the process. Start by finding something you enjoy, and create space in your schedule to practice that thing each day. Make it a priority, and you will eventually make it a habit.

CHAPTER SEVEN

CASE STUDY: THE PROCESS IN ACTION

In the last chapter, we explored tools and tactics to put your action plan into, well, action. We outlined scheduling, habit stacking, and journalling to highlight your process, create consistent practice, and reflect on what works for *you*. I walked you through a bit of my process and how these things have worked (and continue to work) for me. Now, I'm going to walk you through Jane's process—from start to finish.

Jane (whose name is not actually Jane) was one of my first coaching clients. She had recently left her stable 9 to 5 job to begin freelance work from home. Before this shift, a side project of hers quickly gained momentum, and she stepped into a place where she made enough of an income to pursue that project full-time (go, Jane!). But the transition hadn't exactly been a smooth one. As you may know, merely moving offices can stir up chaos! Add all the extra fixings of shifting into self-employment, and things can very quickly feel out of control.

When we worked together, Jane was in her late 20s, no kids, and now worked from home. Due to her recent shift in work, she was investing long, tiring hours into her business and clients, and she lacked the energy to maintain other hobbies and commitments. Her lifestyle lacked boundaries—it became all about work. The more work she put in, the more her business would grow. Jane was highly motivated and passionate about her business but was also extremely aware of this lifestyle imbalance.

What was Jane to do?

Based on what you know about Jane and her current situation, where would you begin? What would you prioritize?

Build a purposeful framework

First things first: Jane needed to set clear parameters for herself. With her previous job, her hours and boundaries were set for her. But as you may know, self-employment is a different ball game!

We began by building a framework. Jane defined productivity and its parameters within her new lifestyle. This process clarified her ideals (for both of us) so that, moving forward, her action plan would be purposeful, personal, and practical—for her existing circumstances and for where she was headed. This also connected Jane to her purpose so that she'd be able to stay focused as she moved forward.

Now, do you remember the three questions I asked you in the very beginning of this book? On the next page, you'll see what happened when I asked Jane those same questions (and why they're so important for building a framework). As you read Jane's responses and process, reflect on your answers and revise as you see fit.

1.   What brought you here?

I wanted to know Jane's history as well as what she wanted from productivity coaching. This question gave Jane the floor to share her current situation and ideals or expectations—according to her. This took out the guesswork for both of us and allowed us to move forward with clarity.

2. What does productivity mean to you?

As we know, each person can have very different definitions and goals when it comes to productivity. This question allowed me to explore Jane's values and priorities and kept us on the same page. It also ensured that the action plan we created together was relevant for her present situation and future ideals.

3. Why is productivity important?

In the very first chapter of this book, we discussed productivity as "purposeful doing." Paying *attention* to your *intention*. Now, I assumed that Jane wanted to set up a framework with boundaries in order to recreate balance in her life. But I needed to know directly from Jane why it was important for her to be more productive. This way, I had a better picture of how to guide and support her. More importantly, *Jane* needed to identify and communicate why it was important to her so she could connect to and stay rooted in that purpose.

Explore the role of self-care

Next, we delved into self-care. We redefined self-care, discussed its role in productivity, and began to identify Jane's starting point. We explored her self-care activities as well as what she had previously done for herself that had fallen to the wayside or was now replaced by work.

By this point we had a two-part focus. First, Jane wanted to be more productive so she could keep doing what she needed to do to grow her business. Second, she wanted to practice self-care to recreate balance and stay fuelled.

Since self-care and productivity go hand-in-hand, this was our key question: how could Jane be more productive by practicing self-care? (Notice that this question doesn't segregate self-care from productivity (i.e., "be more productive *and* practice self-care"). The word "by" shifts self-care from what might be an obligation or overlooked option to being the *catalyst* for productivity.)

In Jane's case, a self-care practice would help her create balance in her life and keep her fuelled to do what she needed to do to grow her business. Therefore, it would make her more productive—in the way that *she's* defined productivity. Ah, the circle of wellness.

Identify the starting point

Speaking of wellness circles, yes, Jane did the wellness wheel exercise. Now, why did we bother with this when Jane was already aware of her lifestyle imbalance? While she knew her occupation section was larger than the rest, Jane didn't yet know where she wanted (or needed) to invest her energy outside of work.

The wellness wheel can be a powerful visual exercise. Many people benefit from physically *seeing* how much they value their network or spirituality, for example, but how little energy they currently have to invest in those areas of their life. I can't count the number of times I've done this exercise with clients who look at their wheel and think (or say), "Whoa, this is not okay" or, "I really need to make some changes here."

Jane and I used this exercise to assess her personal wellness: physical, emotional, rational, spiritual, occupation, and network. We then took her completed wheel and discussed where she wanted to invest her energy. For Jane, it was her physical health and her network. So we explored what that might look like. What meaningful activities would draw even a little bit of extra attention to these areas of her life? What could Jane begin to do to spend time on the areas she wanted to invest in? And Jane created an extensive list.

Let's pause to review what Jane's process has looked like so far:

- She built a purposeful framework by redefining productivity and self-care on her terms (as well as their importance to her)

- She acknowledged her current situation and assessed her starting point by doing the wellness wheel exercise

- She outlined her action plan by (a) choosing one or two areas she wanted to invest in and (b) identifying specific activities she could do to invest her energy there

The process so far has revolved around the big picture—the framework, self-assessment, and planning (i.e., the first five chapters of this book). Next up: practice the process. We funnelled all of this information into practical steps toward immediate, intentional action. (As we move into the next stage, feel free to use each step of Jane's process as a map or reference point for your own.)

Practice the process

This is where we dive into the nitty-gritty stuff to start taking action. In the previous chapter, we explored three different methods to help you move from plan to practice. Here's what those methods looked like for Jane (and maybe they'll look similar for you).

1. Scheduling: create parameters

We began with Jane's schedule. We organized and restructured her days to reflect her priorities and set boundaries. Jane identified her fixed time, and then we designated certain blocks of time to certain activities or modes of work. This actually freed up more time because it prevented Jane from hopping from administrative tasks to email to running errands, all at random times.

Focusing her time also benefited Jane's mental health by creating clarity for herself and her boundaries with clients. As a result, Jane went from working around the clock to having a structure that allowed her to create consistency with clients and to actually stop working when it was time to do so.

Jane and I then looked at her flexible and free time—both within and outside of her work schedule. Now remember, Jane wanted to focus on her physical health and network. For her, this meant attending group classes at a local gym and engaging in healthy activities with friends. She sought out evening exercise classes as a way to physically shift herself, in body *and* mind, from "work mode" to "health mode" or "self mode."

These evening classes quickly took on a greater purpose than just fitness; they allowed Jane to network with healthy individuals and have a set event in her schedule that indicated it was time to step away from work and call it a day. Additionally, having her workouts at a set time gave Jane the added push she needed to avoid distraction during her workday. Needless to say, this step was a game-changer for both Jane's boundaries and her productivity.

After a while, Jane was actually getting *more* work done (and creating better quality work) in a six-hour day instead of her usual 12. She also started eating better, falling asleep earlier, and incorporating stretches and 15-minute yoga sequences into her lunch routines. (Oh, that's right, Jane also stopped working through her lunch break.)

Let's recap Jane's results from incorporating self-care into her schedule:

- Increased boundaries

- Consistency with clients

- Improved mental health

- Increase in focus

- Time- and energy-management

- Decrease in distractions

- Better quality work in less time

- Regular fitness routine

- Healthy network

- Groundwork for additional healthy habits

2. Habit stacking: do one thing regularly

The next step is habit stacking. Jane started with three evening exercise classes each week and was soon up to four. After regularly attending four classes a week for two months, Jane felt ready to add to her routine. She felt she had a grip on her physical health and now wanted to expand her network.

By this time, Jane seemed to have triple the amount of energy than when she first began our coaching sessions. She met more people at her gym and joined local groups for weekend hikes and meet ups.

And guess what happened? Jane's network started investing in her business! She gained clients through these activities and meet ups— the *right* clients. She started working with people who knew she practiced what she preached, and her business quickly gained momentum by word-of-mouth. She gained long-term clients by shifting her work and lifestyle to align with her wants and needs.

Jane achieved amazing results by starting small and stacking her habits. She:

- Made her fitness routine a priority

- Fulfilled her physical needs/goals

- Grew her network organically

- Maintained a regular habit

- Gained confidence

- Increased her energy (dramatically!)

- Lived according to her personal priorities

- Grew her business by word-of-mouth

- Signed on long-term clients

3. Tracking: reflect on your process

It's important to point out that Jane's process wasn't entirely linear (is any growth ever linear?). There were many times when we'd need to backtrack because of a curveball event or default habit (i.e., Jane's readiness for those 12-hour workdays). During those sessions, I'd ask a few hard-hitting questions, and we'd dig deep into Jane's process and the purpose behind what she was doing. The big picture stuff.

Remember, curveballs and old habits *will* arise. While we can try our best to prevent them by staying on top of things, it's just as important to plan for... surprises. Do your best to plan for when X, Y, or Z pop up. How? By getting crystal clear on why you're doing what you're doing.

This is where journalling comes in. Time and time again, journalling proves itself an essential tool in the worlds of productivity and personal growth. From the beginning, I encouraged Jane to keep track of her purpose and productivity. To do so, she answered three questions each evening, seven days a week:

- What did I do for myself today?

- How did this action benefit me?

- How did this action benefit my business?

Together, Jane and I realized how important it was for her to identify how her self-care benefited different areas of her life. She kept track of how it impacted her business so she could observe correlations that would act as major motivators to practice self-care. But, perhaps more importantly, Jane tracked how her self-care benefited her as a *person*, recognizing her facets of existence outside of her occupation.

The results Jane saw from journalling each night were profound. She:

- Created a new healthy habit

- Stayed grounded in her purpose

- Gained clarity on what worked

- Noticed thought patterns

- Aligned her actions to her goals and priorities

- Identified her key motivators

- Improved her ability to solve problems

- Expanded her perspective

- Observed and celebrated her progress!

My initial question when working with Jane was: how could she be more productive by practicing self-care? The process outlined in this chapter shows you how we answered that question and how her business (and health) benefited from each step. The key with Jane—and with everyone, including *you*—is that the progress is in the process. The growth is in the doing, and the success is in the longevity.

By following this process, you take steps to create a plan that will meet your needs and reflect your priorities as you continue to evolve. Life is full of ebbs and flows, and it's important to create a plan and/or practice that can ride those waves with you. As things change, and as you grow, the key is to grow with intention. How do you do this? You use an action plan that's (you guessed it!) purposeful, personal, and practical.

The next chapter is your personal project in which you'll tie all of the steps together for your work and lifestyle needs. Chances are you've done a lot of the work already. You're ready to bring everything together and go through *your* process. It's time to create your self-care action plan and start moving in your right direction.

CHAPTER EIGHT

THE ANSWER: YOUR GUIDE TO PROGRESS

It's your time to shine! If you've done the steps outlined in each chapter, you've already done a *lot* of work on your action plan. Now's your time to lay everything on the table and connect the pieces of your puzzle.

In the framework stage, you defined productivity and self-care for yourself. You identified why these matter to you—the *purpose* behind your process to come. Next, you built awareness and assessed the many facets of your person—your physical, emotional, rational, and spiritual self along with your occupation and network. Using the wellness wheel, you acknowledged your energy investments and determined what self-care and productivity look like within your roles, lifestyle, needs, and wants.

But wait, there's more! The wellness wheel wasn't your project for this book. It was really only the beginning, a determinant for your action plan. I hope you've done your work and are caught up by this point. If you haven't created your definitions, built your framework, or completed your wellness wheel, I encourage you to revisit the previous chapters to do so now. Moving forward without laying the groundwork makes for a pretty shaky road ahead.

Remember, this is your action plan and your process. If you want to be more productive at work and increase your wellness in general, it will take your time and energy. Your wellness is an investment and an essential one at that.

This is the part of the book where you'll create your personal self-care action plan for increased productivity and wellness—at work and otherwise. You know by now that your wellness extends far beyond your desk and job title. You know that the facets that make you *you* are interconnected and that the benefits of self-care weave through those connections (i.e., increased physical or emotional wellness will impact your occupation and network and vice-versa).

The purpose of an action plan is to reduce the guesswork. So instead of having a rough day and having no clue what to do about it or repressing your stress and emotions, you'll have a go-to plan of action. Instead of feeling frustrated, stuck, or uncertain about where you fit in, you'll have a strong purpose and a clear process.

Here's a basic breakdown of what that might look like:

- You'll check in with yourself to identify your current state (i.e., your workflow, stressors, satisfaction, etc.)

- Equipped with a self-care practice, you'll use this to deal with stress, regain clarity, and realign with your priorities

- As a result, you'll gain and maintain the fuel you need to be present and to move forward in a way that is healthy, meaningful, and productive

Sounds simple, right? That's because it can be. Let's explore the ANSWER to reducing guesswork with your action plan:

- **A**wareness

- **N**eeds

- **S**chedule

- **W**hy

- **E**very day

- **R**eview

(Note: the rest of this chapter involves a lot of questions, steps, and reflection. While you can use the space provided on each page to map out the first few steps, I recommend getting ahead of the game with a notebook, journal, or digital document. It's never too early to begin developing the habit of tracking your process!)

Awareness

The first step to creating meaningful change is rooted in inquiry and introspection. Assess your current situation, lifestyle, and self-care practice. This includes building your framework and doing the wellness wheel exercise.

Start by looking at your completed wheel and answering the questions below.

How does the way you currently spend your time and energy affect your productivity?

How will a balanced wheel benefit your work and life in general?

What might your ideal wellness wheel (or lifestyle) look like?

Needs

If you haven't already done so, take a moment to define what you need from your self-care practice. (Feel free to review your self-care definition from chapter two. You can also review your completed wellness wheel and reflect on the areas where you want to spend more energy.)

What do you need from your self-care practice?

Next, hone in on <u>one</u> facet (physical, emotional, rational, spiritual, occupation, or network) to keep your action plan practical and focused. Circle, highlight, or mark your focus area in some way.

What is your area of focus?

Why is it important to you to invest in this area of your life?

Schedule

You've assessed your lifestyle in the form of a wheel; now it's time to look at your day-to-day.

1. Fixed time

Pull out your planner or open your digital calendar, and identify your fixed time: meetings, appointments, lunch breaks, etc. Block off all consistent, ongoing commitments. Start with what you know and move backwards to create parameters and fill in the blanks.

2. Flexible time

Once you've established what's fixed, move on to your flexible time. This includes activities that don't necessarily need to be booked in at a specific time on a certain day. In other words, these are the things that need to get done but that you can move around if you need to (i.e., meal prep, running errands, exercise, etc.). Schedule your activities in where you see fit knowing you can play with the dates and times.

3. Free time

What time do you have that's totally yours? And what do you plan to do with that time? (Hint: use some of it for self-care!)

Consider starting with a 15-minute block for your self-care. Carve out 15 minutes each day at the same time (where possible). Name that block of time whatever you want—self-care, health, personal time, *fun*—and make a note of one to three activities you want to practice (i.e., 15 minutes of yoga before work, a walk during your lunch break, or sitting with a cup of tea and a good book).

Whatever that time looks like, set the appointment. Once it's in there, consider it fixed time and treat it like you would any other meeting or event in your calendar. (I recommend even setting reminders on your phone or computer.)

Reflect on any observations or changes you made to your schedule in order to integrate self-care into your day, week, and life.

Why (+ who, what, when, and where)

These are the specific parameters of your self-care plan. What are doing in your 15-minute time frame to pay attention to your needs? Brainstorm a few ideas, and go through the other W's to refine your activity to be purposeful, personal, and practical for you. Where will you do this activity? With whom? And most importantly, *why* will you do it?

Remember that there's no longevity in "should." This isn't a New Year's resolution or a race to keep up with the Joneses. This is your practice and your process. In order to stick with it, you've got to choose something you actually *want* to do and that will work with your schedule and lifestyle.

Progress comes with practice, and practice comes with purpose. Know your "why."

Keep your "why" at the forefront of your mind. Write it on your wellness wheel, calendar, or, better yet, in your journal. The more visible it is, the more often you'll reflect on it. Staying rooted in your purpose, the reason you started in the first place, helps you get through the tough days and appreciate the good ones. It also ensures that you're growing toward what really matters to you.

Once you've brainstormed a few self-care ideas, take some time to get clear on each one. Consider these questions:

What will you do for yourself?

Why is this important to you?

When will you do this activity?

Where will you do it?

Will you do this activity alone or with someone else? Who?

Every day

This is the doing, the action. Here comes your practice of habit stacking. Start small to create a self-care practice you can do each day. For some, that's 15 minutes of meditation in the morning or journalling in the evening. For others, it could look like a 60-minute exercise class four days a week and 15 minutes of light stretching the other days. It might also be 15 minutes of drawing on your lunch break or half an hour of creative work each evening when you put the kids to bed.

A key point to habit stacking is that your process is qualitative, not quantitative. It's not about the number of hours you put in each week on your activity. The progress is in the process, and your success is in consistent, intentional practice.

This step in your ANSWER is your reminder to be present and to focus on today. *Right now.* If yesterday got away from you, that's okay. Let it go. Revisit the reason you started in the first place, and start again today.

Review

This final (and ongoing) step is where your journal becomes your new best friend. Grab a lined notebook, open a blank document on your computer, or use a journalling app if you so choose. Your medium doesn't matter so long as you keep it consistent.

Start by writing down your purpose for your self-care action plan. Consider exploring these questions:

- Why is self-care important to you?

- What do you hope to gain from a consistent self-care practice?

- How do you envision self-care benefiting you?

Based on your answers, you can determine how you want to use your journal to track your process (and progress). How would you measure the success of your self-care practice? What might you want to look back on six months down the road?

For example, if your purpose is rooted in living a balanced and healthy lifestyle, you might ask:

- What did I do for my health today?

- How did I create more balance in my life?

- How did this action benefit me?

If you're growing a business, you might use Jane's questions from the previous chapter:

- What did I do for myself today?

- How did this action benefit me?

- How did it benefit my business?

Whatever your questions, remember the following:

Keep things simple, and always come back to why you started in the first place.

This is how you'll be consistent in journalling and in your self-care practice. Your journal is your tool to celebrate your efforts and reflect on what works for you and what doesn't (so you can do more of what does!).

And there you have it, there's your ANSWER! It came together pretty quickly, didn't it? It takes regular practice, of course, but the process flows much more smoothly once you've laid the groundwork.

Abraham Lincoln is thought (or perhaps misquoted) to have once said, "Give me six hours to chop down a tree, and I will spend the first four sharpening the axe." By building your framework, identifying your starting point, and outlining your action plan pillars and process, you sharpened your axe so you could cut out the guesswork and reach the root of your personal answer.

All puns aside, by moving through this process, you've now created a purposeful, personal, practical, and *productive* action plan. And it's one that your work, relationships, and health will thank you for.

IN CLOSING

First, I want to recognize the fact that you've asked yourself a lot of vulnerable and perhaps uncomfortable questions throughout this book, and I commend you for taking these important steps toward your productivity and personal wellness. This short book is dense in information and exercises, and I appreciate you sticking it out to the end (and I hope you appreciate you, too!). I hope you recognize and feel empowered by the investment you've made in yourself by going through this process.

I'm grateful to have had this opportunity to share my process and insight as well as your time and energy. I recognize that the last chapter seems abruptly jam-packed with steps. In truth, I could expand each one into its own chapter, but I stuck all of them together *intentionally*. Because, by this point, I think you get it. You've laid your foundation, you know the steps, and you've read specific examples of how to put each one into action. I don't want to weigh you down with more information—the point is to *act*.

As you move through your process, I invite you to use this book as a reference. Come back to its questions, concepts, and handy-dandy acronyms to ensure that your action plan shifts and grows as you do. Use what you've gained—your definitions and framework, the wellness wheel exercise, scheduling, habit stacking, journalling, and any highlighted points—to prioritize and practice what matters to *you*.

Productivity is all about doing the *right* things and doing them well. It's about moving forward in the direction that's right for you. That's my sincere wish for you going forward—wherever your forward leads you.

Stick to the plan you've laid out for yourself in this book, and start living out the specific changes you want to see in your work, your life, and yourself. Each element of your work and each facet of you as a person will thank you.

Remember that you have the knowledge, tools, skills, and, if you've made it this far, the *will* to work and live with purposeful productivity. Know that your progress is in your process and that success lies in consistent and intentional practice. And believe that "should" is nowhere near as powerful as need or want.

Finally, trust in what you know, be patient with yourself, and take things one step at a time.

ABOUT THE AUTHOR

Melissa Steginus is a mindfulness teacher and productivity coach helping people structure their work and lives to be intentional, empowering, and fulfilling. With a background in social work and years of experience as a counsellor, coach, yoga instructor, and world traveller, Melissa has helped thousands of people transform both their personal and professional lives through her workshops, classes, online courses, and individual sessions.

Now living blissfully on the west coast of Canada, Melissa delivers talks and workshops on mindfulness and productivity for clinicians, entrepreneurs, and students of all ages. You can learn more about Melissa, and sign up for her newsletter at: www.melissasteginus.com.

SHARE YOUR CARE

You've learned that your personal well-being doesn't only affect *you*. You have the power (and responsibility) to improve your life, which will also improve the lives of those around you. You help others by taking care of yourself.

Start with *you*. Begin by applying what you've learned to your life. You deserve your own time and attention—not just so you can help others but simply for *you*. You're worth your love.

You can grow from there. Make a list of friends, family members, coworkers, etc. who would benefit from taking better care of themselves—at work and otherwise. Lend them this book or buy them a copy so they can create and live by their own self-care practice.

But promise me you'll take care of *you* first. You'll be amazed by the ripples you create.